IMAGES OF PILGRIMAGE

PARADISE AND WILDERNESS IN CHRISTIAN SPIRITUALITY

R. D. CROUSE

DARTON·LONGMAN+TODD

For they that say such things declare
plainly that they seek a country.

(Hebrews 11:14)

This collection published in 2023 by
Darton, Longman and Todd Ltd
1 Spencer Court
140 – 142 Wandsworth High Street
London SW18 4JJ

Reprinted 2024

ISBN: 978-1-915412-24-9

A catalogue record for this book is available from
the British Library.

Printed and bound in Great Britain by
Bell & Bain, Glasgow

Contents

Preface

This little book had its origin as a series of addresses given to a handful of retreatants at St Augustine's Monastery, Nova Scotia, more than thirty years ago. But like so much that Robert Crouse did, or wrote, or said, its capacity to inspire, by its beauty, depth, and simplicity, is undiminished. I had the privilege of being one of his students, and his voice, his demeanour, his presence, and the inspiration of his deep learning and love feels even closer to me now than it did then.

Robert Darwin Crouse (1930-2011) was a teacher, priest, spiritual director, musician, and gardener. He was also one of the finest theological minds of modern times. The truth of that claim, evident in these meditations, will be further borne out by the volumes that will follow this one. There are indeed few who have his particular gift: introducing us to towering figures like Homer or Augustine or

Dante, and to works of great beauty, like a church in Bominaco or a mosaic in Rome – with at once unassuming gentleness, and immense power, so that these come to life in us, and we discover that 'the love that moves the sun and the other stars' moves in us too.

Fr Crouse was above all a contemplative. He was fond of the story of St Gregory, the sixth-century bishop, who lived in an age of great tumult and chaos, and yet helped to set the shape of Europe, intellectual, moral, and institutional. But how could it be – that out of dissolution, regeneration took hold?

The Venerable Bede had it right, Fr Crouse would say, when he wrote of St Gregory that, 'amid the incessant battering of worldly cares', he strove to be 'fastened, as by the cable of an anchor, to the peaceful shore of prayer' (*Hist. eccl.*, II, I).

Fr Crouse likewise sought communion with the deepest things: to be in his presence was to be in their presence, to sense the 'still centre' amidst the whirl of time and change. That dawning perception – of stillness in the movement of time, of redemption in suffering, of homecoming and liberty in exile and captivity, of, in short, paradise in the wilderness – is indeed what the six addresses of this book bring about. For thinking through these images, images that speak to a universal human reality, is itself a kind of pilgrimage.

Our highest hope is that this little volume, and the volumes of sermons and other writings to follow, will help many to know in their lives here and now, as Fr Crouse and St Gregory did, 'the very life of God Himself'.

Stephen Blackwood

The Works of Robert Crouse

The Works of Robert Crouse is a publishing project that seeks to make the writings and teaching of Fr Robert Crouse available to a contemporary readership seeking guidance and access to the full and abiding tradition of Christian spirituality.

The series will publish three additional volumes in the next year. Two volumes of sermons, *The Soul's Pilgrimage: The Theology of the Christian Year* and *The Soul's Pilgrimage: The Descent of the Dove and the Spiritual Life,* will be followed by *A Theology of Pilgrimage*, a volume of theological essays drawing on our theological tradition to address contemporary issues. These volumes will be followed by a commentary on

Dante's *Divine Comedy*, a work central to Fr Crouse's spiritual vision. Accessible, scholarly, pastoral, tightly argued, philosophically astute, and beautifully written, these writings speak profoundly to the tensions — sacred and profane — that are inherent in our divided and distracted culture pointing us to that hope that can alone bring reconciling justice.

Stephen Blackwood, Neil Robertson, Gary Thorne
Series Editors

Original Preface

T his little book contains the addresses given during the Clergy Retreat of the Diocese of Nova Scotia, at St Augustine's Monastery, in Monastery, Antigonish County, Nova Scotia, in June 1986. They were, of course, designed to be heard in the context of devotional exercises, and not to be read; but at the request of some of the retreatants, I have agreed to have them printed in their original form, with the addition of a few footnotes to acknowledge my sources, and suggest further reading.

In this sixteen-hundredth anniversary year of the conversion of St Augustine, upon whose works these meditations have drawn so heavily, it seems particularly appropriate to dedicate these pages to the Reverend Prior, Fr Isidor, and his colleagues in the order of St Augustine, at Monastery, who have so often, and so graciously, been hosts to these retreats; and to the Reverend Canon Karl Tufts, who has been, for nearly a quarter of a century, the chief organiser and promoter of retreats for the clergy of the diocese.

R. D. C.

Feast of St Augustine, 1986

CHAPTER I

Biblical and Pagan Images

The fundamental and all-encompassing theme of spiritual life is pilgrimage: its images are the images of wayfaring, of exile and repatriation, of alienation and reconciliation, images of journeying through wilderness to gain the promised land. The Bible abounds in imagery of that kind, from the beginning to the end; from man's ancient exile from the paradise of Eden in the Book of Genesis, to the vision of the New Jerusalem in the Book of Revelation. Indeed, the Scriptures represent the whole of our existence, the whole of natural and spiritual life, under images of pilgrimage: from the descent of all things from God in creation, to their return to him in the final summing up of hell and heaven. The theme is all-inclusive, and cosmic in dimension. As St Paul explains 'the whole creation groaneth and travaileth in pain together until now … awaiting the adoption', when 'the creation itself also shall be delivered from the bondage of corruption into the glorious liberty of the children of God' (Rom. 8:19 - 23).

Pilgrimage – pilgrimage to glory, pilgrimage to liberty – is the life of all creation, and the meaning of all natural and human history.

The work of God for man's redemption is represented, too, in just such imagery: the descent of God the Son into the world to do the Father's will, and his return, through a wilderness of suffering and deprivation, to the homeland of the Father's glory; the descent of God the Spirit upon the infant Church, giving unity and order to the chaos of conflicting tongues, and the return of God the Spirit in the Church's life of charity, of penitence and adoration, making intercession 'with groanings that cannot be uttered' (Rom. 8:26).

Finally, in a difficult and profoundly important sense, pilgrimage is the very life of God himself, the Holy Trinity: the outgoing of God the Father in his own self-knowing, which is the eternal begetting of his Word; and the eternal procession of God the Holy Spirit, whereby the knower and the known are bound in mutual love. Thus, the very name of God, as love, bespeaks the timeless pilgrimage of God. What, then, is man's imaging of God, but a timely imitation of that eternal pilgrimage? What is man's vocation, but the call to take the pilgrim's way, to be caught up in the drawing of that supernal triune love which (as Dante puts it) 'moves the sun and the other stars'?[1]

The whole of revelation is encompassed by the images of pilgrimage, of wilderness and paradise. It is possible, of course, to translate those images into the more precise, explicit language of theology – to 'demythologise' the images – and we may attempt something of the sort from time to time; but mainly, I think, we should stay close to the language of the images themselves. That is, after all, the primary form of revelation, and although the precisions of theology are important and necessary, the images have a depth and richness, or wholeness, which the exactness and explicitness of scientific language can never quite exhaust.[2]

Consider, for instance, so simple a composition as a few lines of an old 'spiritual', which move entirely on the plane of biblical imagery:

I looked over Jordan an' what did I see,
Comin' for to carry me home?
A band of angels, comin' after me,
Comin' for to carry me home.

What is being said there? Nothing, really, is explained, yet everything is said, in the wonderful play of images.

'I looked over Jordan': the pilgrim people stand at the border of the promised land, looking with eager, yearning eyes towards the place of liberty and peace, longing for the fulness of salvation. Behind them lies the bondage of Egypt, and the miracle of Exodus; the forty years of weary wandering; the pillar of cloud by day, and the pillar of fire by night; manna from the skies, and water from the stony rock; fiery serpents to scourge, and the brazen serpent to heal; laws and prophecies, and fears and hopes; all that, and so much more, lies behind those yearning eyes.

'I looked over Jordan.' The river is the last frontier, the border between the wilderness and paradise, the border which only faith can cross. It is the mystery of water: floods that either overwhelm or fructify; waters of destruction and regeneration, death and re-birth; water of baptism; waters that 'make glad the city of God' (Ps. 46:5); all that, and more, is there.

'I looked over Jordan, an' what did I see?' The eyes of faith, purified and chastened in the wilderness, clarified through suffering and deprivation, can look across the border and see divine deliverance: 'A band of angels, comin' after me.' I cannot cross the river by myself; only God can give salvation, only God can 'carry me home'. The angels are his messengers and messages: angels, who rejoice over every sinner who repents; messengers of God – all the beneficent powers and virtues of nature and of grace, revealed and given in the Gospel of the Saviour, 'comin' for to carry me home'. 'Home' is where the heart is; the place of freedom and security, the Father's mansion, to which the Prodigal returns from wandering in barren places.

All that, and so much more, is contained in, and evoked by, those few, simple lines, by virtue of the richness and the interplay of divinely-given images. These are images of pilgrimage, and each one suggests and calls to mind a host of others. One could explain for hours, and still not be much below the surface. There is always something more there, something new and fresh to be seen there. Such is the language of revelation, the language of liturgy and prayer. That language is not just *about* pilgrimage: the understanding of the language, the penetration of the images, is itself a kind of pilgrimage. God is not, finally, other than his Word; and to penetrate the images, to see through them to their very ground, will be to see God face to face in the life of paradise. God's word may seem a wilderness of words; but its images are translucent, and his word becomes a paradise of light and life.[3]

The substance of our meditations will be the images of pilgrimage, of paradise and wilderness, as they are found in Holy Scripture; and St Augustine and Dante will provide us with two eminent examples of the fecundity of those images for the Christian mind. But, just before we venture on that quest, I want to do something which may strike you as a diversion.

∼

Images of pilgrimage are not only biblical and Christian; they are universal. As historians of religion, and historians of art and literature have fully demonstrated, such images inform the consciousness and aspirations of every human culture, from the most primitive to the most sophisticated, in modern as well as in ancient times, in every quarter of the globe.[4] Whether we explain this fact according to an ancient Platonic theory of 'recollection', or a modern Jungian theory of the 'collective unconscious' (which are perhaps not, after all, so very different), or in some other way, the phenomenon, at least, is evident: these images belong somehow to the essence of our humanity; they are essential and permanent features of our spiritual landscape, whether secular or sacred. And even if we deny the images, and seek to banish them, and lose ourselves in immediate occupations, still they impinge upon our consciousness, in the sense of emptiness and futility they leave behind them. By our very denial, we somehow affirm them.

The images are universal, and belong essentially to the human consciousness; they are not only biblical and Christian. The similarities are striking and profound. But even more significant are certain crucial differences. I think that we can better understand both the likenesses and the differences, if we first establish some context of comparison, and for that reason, although it might seem to be a diversion, I want to explore first some images of pilgrimage in pagan culture; specifically in the spirituality of ancient, pagan Greece and Rome.

I think that will be the most useful comparison, for several reasons: first, because in that pagan culture, we find a spirituality developed to a very high degree, richly articulated in artistic and literary forms, and thoroughly interpreted; secondly, because (as we shall see with St Augustine) it was in relation to that culture that the distinctive claims of Christianity were sharply clarified; and thirdly, because it is towards that pagan spirituality that we ourselves are drawn when we forget our Christianity. Historically, Christianity both assumes and rejects that ancient paganism. There is no St Augustine without the pagan Platonists though he is their severest critic;[5] and there is no Dante without Aristotle and Virgil, though he is compelled to consign the great philosopher, '*il maestro di color che sanno*' – 'the master of those who know' – together with his beloved poet, everlastingly to Limbo, the state of frustrated aspiration.[6] His pain and gentleness in doing so makes one of the most moving episodes, I think, in all of Dante's poetry.

I think that we, too, must have some sense of the nobility and tragedy of paganism, if we would understand the glory and the liberating force of the images of biblical and Christian spirituality. And therefore, I ask you to follow me, for a brief space, into the literature of ancient Greece and Rome.

Fundamental in that literature are the images

of pilgrimage: the *odos* – the road that lies before us, the journey, and the *agon* – the hero's struggle through a wilderness of one sort or another, to find a reconciliation, a paradise, which is eternal and divine. Homer, sometimes called 'the Bible of the Greeks', sets the tone of this heroic pilgrimage, most obviously in the *Odyssey*, the great epic poem about Odysseus, the wayfarer, the pilgrim (that is what his name means), as he makes his homeward way from ruined Troy to Ithaca. His wilderness is a wilderness of sea and islands (the 'wine-dark sea', presided over by unfriendly Poseidon, but still within the providence of Zeus), through which he makes his way, beset by peril, trials and temptation, hungering for home.

It is a wonderful adventure story; but it is also more than that: it embodies a profound spiritual lesson, one which holds the essence of all pagan tragedy; and most astutely does Aristotle identify Homer as the first of the tragedians. Consider how the story ends: Odysseus, finally returned to Ithaca, slaughters the suitors of his wife, Penelope; and when their sons and brothers come upon him to avenge their deaths, he proceeds to slaughter them relentlessly, and his hand is stayed only by the intervention of Athena, who (says Homer):

19

... cast a grey glance at her friend, and said: 'Son of Laertes and the gods of old, Odysseus, master of land ways and sea ways, command yourself. Call off this battle now, or Zeus who views the wide world may be angry'.[7]

The point is just this: the hero must learn what are the human limitations, and moderate his zeal. His thirst is for a completeness, the divine realm, 'the wide world' which belongs to Zeus alone. Precisely in heroic aspiration lies the tragic flaw, the hero's *hubris* – the overweening pride which knows no finite limits; really, the satanic temptation to 'be as gods, knowing good and evil', having the whole in one's possession. '*Gnothi seauton*' said the oracle at Delphi, 'know thyself'; know that you are a man, and not a god, and be content with human limitations.

There is the essence of the tragic view of life: heroic virtue, heroic aspiration, *is* heroic *hubris*, and is destined for defeat. That is the worm at the heart of pagan spirituality: the endless cycles of aspiration and despair. There is an *odos*, a road of pilgrimage, a journey through a wilderness of suffering, but that road turns back upon itself, and ends in contradiction. Dante rightly sees that the conclusion of the *Odyssey* is really no conclusion; that heroic virtue cannot abide the limitation; and therefore, he provides a sequel (apparently his own invention), in which he attributes to Odysseus one final, disastrous assault upon Mount Purgatory, the Earthly Paradise.[8]

Illustrations could be multiplied indefinitely from the poets, the religious movements, and the philosophers of ancient pagan culture. The philosophers speak, of course, a somewhat different language, but the message is the same: the gulf between the pure and perfect good of paradise, which is divine, and the realities of human life, is eternally unbridgeable. The divine good, says Aristotle, is 'a life too high for man', though, at the same time, it is the only end of human longing, and man's only final happiness.[9] There is that in man which is divine, and man will be satisfied with nothing less. The pilgrimage is both necessary and impossible. That is the tragic contradiction.

One more illustration seems especially important, if only because it lies so directly in the background of both St Augustine and Dante. That is from the Roman poet, Virgil. In the sixth book of the *Aeneid*, Aeneas, under the auspices of the prophetic Sibyl, makes a journey to the underworld, the place of the departed, to the fields of Elysium (the place of liberty), where he converses with his own departed father, Anchises. Aeneas is much puzzled to see a multitude of souls gathered at the border of the river Lethe, the waters of forgetfulness. Anchises explains that all these souls, pure spirits, sparks of elemental fire, must drink these waters of oblivion, so that they may endure, once more, to enter into the fetters of the body, to be hampered once again by the body's evils.

> Each of us finds the world of death fitted to himself. Then afterwards we are released to go free about wide Elysium, and we few possess the fields of joy, until length of days, as time's cycle is completed, has removed the hardened corruption, and leaves, without taint now, a perception pure and bright, a spark of elemental fire. Now when these souls have trodden the full circle of a thousand years, God calls all of them forth in long procession to Lethe river, and this he does so that when they again visit the sky's vault, they may be without memory, and a wish to re-enter bodily life may dawn.[10]

Then Aeneas returns to earthly life, and, says Virgil, he returns through the gate of ivory; the gate through which the spirits send the visions which are false in the light of day.

Just what is being said there? One must aspire to paradise, the place of joy and liberty, the place of pure and perfect good, the divine life. But that is God's life; for man, it is a false dream which spirits send through gates of sleep. To possess the earth, and content oneself with it, one must drink the waters of oblivion, and forget Elysium. One must find substitutes, of course: the most potent was the pious fiction that the Empire was eternal, and the Emperor divine. A fiction, certainly; and surely one knew it was a fiction. But it was a spiritually necessary fiction, and really no less plausible than the similarly necessary fictions of modern paganism.

'Idolatry', cried the Christians, and, of course, they were absolutely right. But then, idolatry in one form or another is all that one has left when one despairs of the pilgrimage to God. The comment of St Gregory the Great, looking back on Roman history, seems to me profoundly perceptive. Speaking of the reign of Trajan, whom he much admired, and those days of imperial prosperity, he says: 'In their hearts, it had already withered.' [11]

From a pagan standpoint, the pure and perfect good, the divine life, is the deepest longing, the highest aspiration, of the human spirit; but alas, its conclusion is impossible; it is a life too high for man. That has nothing to do with any moral failure of ours. There is nothing voluntary about it, it is simply the nature of things. The distance is too great, there can be no mediation. That is just the way things are, have always been, and always will be, and we had best content ourselves with that. To insist on more than that is folly, the flaw of *hubris*, the tragic flaw; it goes too far.

Dante can blame Odysseus, and with a stroke of sheer poetic brilliance, give his story a conclusion, and place him far down in the 'Inferno', in the circle of the fraudulent.[12] But that judgement is possible only from a Christian standpoint. From a pagan point of view, there is really nothing essentially voluntary in the situation of Odysseus. As Homer's Alcinous tells Odysseus, 'That was all gods' work, weaving ruin there so it would make a song for men to come'.[13] The predicament is simply there, in the nature of things. Zeus has two urns, and pours from both, combining good and evil.[14] The philosophers draw back from that conclusion: Plato denies the duplicity of Zeus, and insists that 'the fault is his who chooses'.[15]

But then, as one sees in Plato's 'Myth of Er',

the choice is limited; one cannot really choose the paradise of God, but only among better and worse finite alternatives.[16] The *impasse* remains.

We must ever keep an upward course, we must cultivate the virtues, and be disciplined by suffering; but we must know that, in the end, there really is no end, no final paradise for us. That is the nature of things, the everlasting order of the universe. We can make our idols, to be sure, our eternal empires and universal panaceas; but we cannot but suspect that they have feet of clay, and when we see that, the issue is despair. That is the essence, I think, of that pagan 'futility of mind' of which St Paul speaks in his Letter to the Romans.[17]

It is against the background of that spiritual *impasse* that we should begin to look at some aspects of biblical spirituality in the Old Testament images of paradise and wilderness.

CHAPTER II

The Old Testament

As we approach the images of pilgrimage in the Holy Scriptures of the Old Testament, there is, to begin with, much that should be said about the creation narrative with which the Book of Genesis begins.[18]

Historically, the understanding of Genesis has often been regarded as the fundamental starting point of Christian spirituality. We still possess, for instance, the series of Lenten lectures on that subject by St Basil of Caesarea, delivered to the catechumens as they prepared for Easter baptism. We have a similar series from St Ambrose. Genesis was used, in ancient Christianity, as a basic text for the instruction of the neophytes. The last three books of St Augustine's *Confessions*, his beginning of meditation on the texts of Scripture, are devoted to the creation narrative, as are several other substantial treatises by him. The Venerable Bede set himself the same task, as did also the great ninth-century philosopher, John Scotus Eriugena; and in the twelfth century, that great age of European spiritual awakening, commentaries on the creation story were abundant.[19]

We might ask ourselves why, among all the rich treasures of divine revelation, that particular story should have been regarded as so vitally important. Certainly, in modern times, it can still stir up some interest, especially in controversies between 'creationists' and 'evolutionists'. But that is an interest of a very different sort, and it is, I think, essentially frivolous, so far as that passage is concerned, because it misses the point of what the text is all about. I hope we can agree that what we have there is not some primitive geophysical hypothesis, but something very different, and of immeasurably greater import.

We may debate about the text, whether it should be understood historically or allegorically, or both; and, if historically, in just what sense that might be so. That was a question already much discussed in ancient times by both Jews and Christians. Problems about historicity, and what historicity might mean, are by no means new. St Augustine, among others, has extensive and very useful treatments of such questions. Still, those questions were not, and are not, the fundamental issue. The core of Christian interest in the text, and the reason for its place in early Christian education, lies rather in the fact that in that passage are established, once for all, the foundations of biblical and Christian spirituality. These are the sign-posts, the basic terms and principles, of the spirit's pilgrimage. That is why those lessons were expounded to the catechumens: it was those lessons which first and decisively marked the border which they crossed as they moved from paganism to Christianity.

The first, and most obvious, lesson is simply this: all existence is in the Word of God. 'He spake and it was done.' All is divine utterance: 'He commanded, and they were created.' All things are in and by God's word; there is nothing else there. And the breath of God, his Holy Spirit, moves through all things, *fortiter et suaviter* – 'firmly and unhindered' – as the arrangement and adornment of the whole. There is nothing outside that: no dark and doubtful element, no 'errant cause', no truculence of nature. Each thing, taken severally, is good; all things, taken in their ordered whole, are very good. They are the word and breath of

God. 'By the word of the Lord were the heavens made, and all the hosts of them by the breath of his mouth': the word and breath; the Word and Spirit of the Father. 'The morning stars sang together, and all the sons of God shouted for joy.'

All this is represented, encapsulated, so to speak, in the image of paradise – the garden of innocent delight, planted eastward in Eden. It is a garden which (*mirabile dictu!*) has no weeds; thorns and thistles are a certain aftermath. It is presumptuous to say that the paradisal image is superb: every line of it is weighted with significance. Adam, image and similitude of God, created in the Father's Word and Spirit, is created there in that garden of delight, 'to dress it and to tend it', work which is not labour (there is as yet no sweat upon his brow); work which is image of divine activity. In his naming and his governing of every creature in the garden, in his knowing and his care, man is image of Father, Word and Spirit; he is nature's priest, divine image, reflecting back, offering up, the Word and Spirit of the Lord.

There is nothing there in actuality which is not the word and will of God; nothing there which is not simply good. What, then, about that tempting tree of the knowledge of good and evil? What of the wicked serpent? What of rebelling angels? They are signs and symbols of the potencies of will; they are there, and must be there, if will is to be will. Thus it is that they 'present' themselves, in the image of the serpent. The mystery of temptation there is not some dark and evil element in the nature of reality; it is the mystery of that liberty which belongs to all good will. In that sense, it is God's creation. The serpent will wound, but the brazen serpent in the wilderness will heal. There can be nothing in creation which is not God's, nothing unencompassed by his providence, nothing which falls outside his word and will.

We cannot make, nor can we unmake, paradise; it is the fundamental reality of things, abiding in the word and will of God. We cannot make it, nor can we destroy it. To suppose so is mere foolishness. It abides; it is given. When the kingdom comes, it comes from God: the Holy City, paradise, descends from God out of heaven, because that is where it always is.[20] We cannot touch the purity, the holiness, of that; we can only turn our eyes away, and lose ourselves in a wilderness of unreality. That is our expulsion from the garden. That is what the thorns and thistles are about, and the reason of our sweat.

Paradise abides, even when our eyes do not

look upon it, and our home is always there; when we return, it is to that home. That is why biblical and Christian spirituality always involves *conversio* – 'conversion', repentance, turning back, to find, in the end, what is really our beginning. It is the return to paradise, to Eden; but it is also something more than that, for in returning, we come to know the place in a new way. We come to know it for the first time. Our wilderness is not outside the providence of God, and it is in that wilderness that we learn to mark the lineaments of paradise.

In the wilderness, the image of paradise becomes prophetic image. Consider, for instance, how Isaiah evokes that imagery:

> The Lord shall comfort Zion: he will comfort all her waste places; and he will make her wilderness like Eden, and her desert like the garden of the Lord; joy and gladness shall be found therein, thanksgiving and the voice of melody. (Is. 51:3)

And, later on:

> The wolf and the lamb shall feed together, and the lion shall eat straw like the bullock;

and dust shall be the serpent's meat. They
shall not hurt nor destroy in all my holy
mountain, saith the Lord. (Is. 65:25)

It is an evocation of the paradisal harmony of
Eden, and also something more; wilderness has
given new dimension to the image. Paradise is not
simply return to Eden, it is *forma futuri*,[21] a sign of
what is to come: 'For behold, I create new heavens
and a new earth' (65:17). The image of Eden is
conflated with the vision of the city of Jerusalem
renewed: 'I create Jerusalem a rejoicing, and her
people a joy' (65:18). In prophecy, the image of
the garden becomes the image of the redeemed
city.

The images of pilgrimage, of paradise and
wilderness, specify totally the spirituality of the
Old Covenant. Everywhere, the same thing is
implied: it is there in the call of Abraham, who
takes a strange road, which is really the road home;
it is there in the great epic of Israel's exile and
return from Egypt to the Promised Land, recalled
as present and prophetic reality in the ritual of
Passover; it is there in the Babylonian captivity,
and the rebuilding of the temple in Jerusalem. And
what are laws and sacrifices, but intimations of the

way, *formae futuri*, signs of what is coming; images seen as in a clouded mirror? These biblical images may usefully be compared with those belonging to the ancient pagan world, and in order to sharpen the comparison, I wish to introduce just one more, from the poetry of Virgil, from the 'Fourth Eclogue': a text so striking in its likeness to the story of the paradise of Eden that it was sometimes supposed that Virgil must have been a Christian prophet.[22]

The poet has a vision of the lost 'golden age', and looks to its return. It is the age of perfect, paradisal bliss, a harmony of man and nature. The earth brings forth its fruits without man's sweat and labour; the soil need never feel the hoe. The sheep upon the hillsides spontaneously dye their own wool. Greed and competition vanish from the earth; the infant monarch comes, and the age of peace, the golden age, returns once more to earth. Even now, the fates are spinning: 'Run, spindles, run' – and it will come to pass. It is the ever-flowing, ever-ebbing work of fate.

We may put that in more prosaic terms: paradise is an ideal, one of the alternatives, in the ebb and flow of which our life is lived. It is fated. That is to say, that ebb and flow belong to the nature of things, in their very constitution. One may speak the language of fate, or not; the point is that both sides are there in the nature of things.

Against a background such as that, what did the Christians mean when they gave their catechumens the text of Genesis as a new and different spirituality? For Genesis, as we have seen, paradise is not one of the alternatives, fated, in the nature of things. It is the one reality of things, in the word and will of God. Our exile from paradise is not our fate; it is our will which freely turns away to unreality, and makes our life a barren wilderness. The alternatives are not just there in nature. As St Augustine put it (in conscious opposition to Roman paganism), two 'cities' are founded by two loves: one love which looks to the reality of God; and another which turns away to self, and makes our world a dismal fantasy. [23]

Further, the spirituality of the Bible is profoundly social; it is not the pilgrimage of the hero, but of a people. From the beginning, it is not just Adam, it is man and woman. It is their children, Cain and Abel; it is the seed of Abraham; it is the flock of Israel. Paradise is a city, the New Jerusalem. As St Augustine says, in the *City of God*, 'Whence could this city originate, or pursue its course, or come to its

34

appointed end, were the life of the saints not a social life?'.[24]

It would not do to suggest that the spirituality of paganism is in no sense social. Virgil's golden age is social, and, after all, does not the *polis*, the city, have a fundamental place in the spirituality of ancient Greece? Consider the high doctrine of Aristotle's *Politics*: the form of the state is the form of *philia*, the form of friendship, which is the form of all the virtues. Yet, there is an incompleteness about that friendship; God must be outside it, for the distance is too great between divine and human life.[25] *Philia* approaches, but cannot yet be transfigured into charity.[26]

State *cultus*, state religion, persists throughout the ancient pagan world, right up to the end; but increasingly, from the time of Plato on, the vitality of religion is not really there. It lives in the proliferation of private cults – the mystery cults – which promise experience of religion in their initiation rites. Thus, in paganism, religion becomes a matter of multiplicity of cult, and essentially a private thing, a matter of individual 'experience'.[27]

It follows from these points that the virtues of the pilgrim of paradise must be very different from the virtues of the pagan hero. The boldness, the cunning craftiness of Odysseus will not do; not even the *pietas*, the steadfast moral determination of Aeneas will do; the virtues of the pilgrim must be obedience and humility. I must wait upon God 'to carry me home'.

CHAPTER III

The New Testament

As we begin to think about images of pilgrimage, of paradise and wilderness, in the Scriptures of the New Testament, we can put aside, for a time, our pagan comparisons, for the point of comparison will now be the Old Testament; and to that end, we should take up more fully the meaning of Old Testament images of wilderness. [28]

The spiritual meaning of wilderness becomes especially clear, of course, in the story of the Exodus. Yet, there remains a remarkable ambiguity in that meaning. Wilderness is both curse and blessing: it is the place where fiery serpents lurk to wound, but it is also the place where the brazen serpent is lifted high to heal; it is the dry and barren land where people starve, but it is also where the gift is made, of supernatural food from heaven. It is the place of lawlessness, but it is also the place where the law of God is given and received. It is in the wilderness, the place of solitude, that God speaks thunderingly; and it is there that the tribes of Israel come to know themselves as chosen people.

When they forget their calling, and turn their eyes again towards Egypt, they must learn again the lesson of the wilderness, in the exile in Babylon, which is a spiritual analogue of wilderness. Ezekiel calls it, explicitly, 'the wilderness of the peoples': 'I will bring you into the wilderness of the peoples', says his prophecy, 'and there I will enter into judgement with you face to face' (Ez. 20:35, 36). See the ambiguity of that: only in the strange land will Israel discern the word and will of Israel's God.

> By the waters of Babylon we sat down and wept, when we remembered thee, O Sion …
>
> How shall we sing the Lord's song in a strange land? (Ps. 137)

But only in that wilderness could the Lord's song be renewed, and only from the wilderness could Sion, the house of God, be rebuilt. As Rilke puts it, in his strangely beautiful way:

Only whoso has raised among the shades his
lyre dares, with foreboding, aspire to offer
infinite praise. [29]

As we approach the New Testament, especially
in that remarkable non-canonical, sectarian, and
apocalyptic literature which both pre-dates and
surrounds the Christian writings, we find the theme
intensified. The *Apocalypse of Baruch* may speak for all:

The shepherds of Israel have perished, and
the lamps which gave light are extinguished,
and the fountains have withheld their stream
from which we used to drink. And we are
left in darkness, and amidst the briars of the
forest, and the thirst of the wilderness.

But the wilderness will be redeemed, in the age
of the Messiah, and the prophet represents that
redemption with a conflation of the images of
wilderness and Eden:

And it will come to pass at that self-same
time that the treasury of manna will again
descend from on high, and they who have
persevered in righteousness will eat of it in

those years … And wild beasts will come from the forest and minister unto men, and asps and dragons will come forth from their holes, and submit themselves to a little child. [30]

Not only is the positive significance of wilderness intensified, but images of wilderness and paradise (Eden) tend towards a conflation. Paradise and wilderness are to be one; paradise is to be the wilderness transfigured.

Those curious non-canonical documents, and the ascetical wilderness communities which produced them (e.g., Essenes, Qumran), stand just around the fringes of the New Testament, and it is St John the Baptist who takes us across that borderline. Just what he may have had to do with any such communities, we may perhaps never know; but he is clearly one of those who prepare in the wilderness a highway for the Lord. John comes, baptizing, to Bethabara, 'beyond Jordan' (St John, 1:28): that is to say, in the wilderness, on the border of the Promised Land. It is there that God is to be met with face to face; it is there that his coming will be recognised. And in his coming, the law, 'all righteousness', will be fulfilled. Paradise and wilderness will be identified.

The Gospels abound in just such conflated imagery. Consider just a few examples: Jesus goes, driven by the Spirit, to the wilderness, where he undergoes forty days of fasting, echoing the fast of Moses, and the forty years of Israel's privations, and there, once more, the covenant is clarified: 'Thou shalt not tempt the Lord thy God'. 'Thou shalt worship the Lord thy God, and him only shalt thou serve.' And then the wilderness is no more satanic: 'Angels came and ministered unto him.' Wilderness becomes paradise. [31]

And consider the miracles of feeding. 'How can anyone satisfy these men with bread here in the wilderness?' The miraculous bread is explicitly related to the ancient gift of manna in the desert; but this manna, now, is indeed the food of paradise. It is the Lord himself who comes from heaven. This bread is, even now, eternal life. Once again, wilderness is paradise.

We might consider, too, the paradisal imagery of Pentecost. 'They spake with other tongues, as the Spirit gave them utterance', and all the strangers, from foreign parts, understood, as though it were each one's own language. It is, of course, the reversal of the confusion of tongues which punished the architects of the ancient tower of Babel. That story of the tower is another image of the fall of Man; of the expulsion from paradise. The similarity to the Eden story is in some ways very striking. In Eden, the temptation is to 'be as gods'; with the tower of Babel, it is the same thing – the attempt to take heaven as one's own possession. At Pentecost, the wilderness of tongues – language at its most confused, language which is apparent nonsense – becomes the harmonic speech of paradise. Paradise and wilderness are conflated.

The heart of the matter is to be found in the Last Supper discourse, in St John's Gospel, where Jesus teaches his disciples the meaning of his departure and return:

> Verily, I say unto you, that ye shall weep and lament, but the world shall rejoice; and ye shall be sorrowful, but your sorrow shall be turned into joy. A woman, when she is in travail, hath sorrow, because her hour is come: but as soon as she is delivered, she remembereth no more the anguish, for joy that child is born into the world. And ye now therefore have sorrow; but I will see you again, and your heart shall rejoice,

and your joy no man taketh from you
(Jn 16:20-22).

The point is just this: the wilderness of desolation
becomes the paradise of joy; physical departure
becomes spiritual presence; they are inseparable;
there is no one without the other. All this comes
into focus with the Cross, which is at once the tree
of utter desolation, and the tree of glory; the tree
of death, and the tree of life. It is the tree which
lifts the brazen serpent in the wilderness, and the
tree of paradise, whose leaves are for the healing
of the nation. What was, for the pagan hero, tragic
contradiction – 'foolishness to the Greeks'; what
was, for the people of the Old Covenant, shrouded
in ambiguity – 'a stumbling block to the Jews'; is
here reconciled and clarified, as 'the power of God
and the wisdom of God'.

The inspired imagination which identifies the
Cross with the paradisal tree of life penetrates to
profound truth. You will all recall what wonderful
things Fortunatus does with that imagery in his
hymns on the Holy Cross. Perhaps some of you
may know the great mosaic which adorns the
apse of the Church of San Clemente, in Rome.
There, in the centre, is the Cross, clearly the tree

of life, planted upon the hill of paradise restored by Christ. From the base, there flow four streams, to water paradise, and harts are drinking from the streams. There are doves, representing souls, and the phoenix of immortality. The tree is at the same time a vine ('Let us liken the Church of Christ to this vine', says the inscription), which spreads its branches to give life to all creation. Over the tree is the hand of God the Father; in a border at the bottom are the twelve apostles, represented as lambs, flanking the Lamb of God in the centre of the border. Images of Eden, of the Cross, and of the Church's life are all gathered there in a magnificent conflation. [32]

Obviously, a certain spiritual tension is represented in the conflation of the biblical images, and it is a tension inherent in Christian spirituality as represented in the New Testament. It is the tension expressed, for instance, in the apparent contradiction between 'realised' and 'futurist' eschatology. With the coming of the Son of Man, the Kingdom comes: it is here for you, it is within your reach, it is within you; and that is paradise. But the Son of Man is also yet to come in glory: not in a secret wilderness out there, but here, and everywhere; 'for as the lightening cometh out of the east, and shineth even unto the west; so shall the coming of the Son of Man be' (Mt. 24:17).

In the New Testament, the spiritual tension of the 'interim' is expressed in several ways. In the Johannine literature, it is expressed principally in terms of love. The eternal life of paradise is present here and now, because we know the love of God: 'we have known and believed the love that God hath to us' (I John, 4:16), the love manifested in the sending of the only begotten Son, that we might live through him. 'We have passed from death to life'; we have entered paradise; 'because we love the brethren' (3:14). Love of brethren is the sign of the life of paradise, and the precise reversal of the enmity of Cain towards Abel. 'He that dwelleth in love dwelleth in God, and God in him' (4:16). Fear is cast out, and there is no sin. Here, truly, is the life of paradise. Yet, the fact remains that love must be commanded (4:21), and law belongs to wilderness. Paradise is in this wilderness; the two are conflated, but not simply so: this is paradise for those who will discern the signs, and live in obedience to them.

In the Pauline literature, exactly the same spiritual tension is present, in the most fundamental way, though in a somewhat different language. Many familiar Pauline phrases dramatically express that tension. Here are some examples, selected rather at random: 'Work out your own salvation in fear and trembling' (there is the wilderness), 'for it is God which worketh in you, both to will and to do of his good pleasure' (there is paradise) (Phil. 2:12-13); 'Our conversation is in heaven' (there is paradise); 'from whence also we look for the Saviour' (there is wilderness) (Phil. 3:20). Such examples could be multiplied; those oppositions belong to the tension which marks the Pauline theology of law and grace, of justification and sanctification. 'Being justified by faith, we have peace with God through our Lord Jesus Christ' (Rom. 5:1). All is done, all has been accomplished; yet 'the inward man is renewed day by day', as we look towards the unseen, eternal things (II Cor. 4:16-18). Amid temptations to be conformed to the spirit of the present age, we seek renewal of the mind (Rom. 12:3), as we await our conformation to the image of the Son, 'from glory to glory, even as by the Spirit of the Lord' (II Cor. 3:18). 'Now we see through a glass, darkly; but then face to face' (I Cor.13:12). Wilderness and paradise stand in opposition; it is charity, the Spirit's gift (Rom. 5:5), which binds the two together, in a single peace. Thus, we 'rejoice in hope', and 'glory in tribulations' (Rom. 5:2-3), knowing 'that all things work together for good to them that love God, to them that are called according to his purpose' (Rom. 8:28).

It is in that spiritual tension between commandment and love, between law and grace, between 'the present age' and 'the age to come' (both of which are present), between wilderness and paradise (present together), that Christian spirituality makes its pilgrimage. It is that tension which necessarily characterizes the spiritual life of the Christian Church, historically, as we shall see in our meditations on the works of St Augustine and Dante.

CHAPTER IV

St Augustine

P assing on to consider the interpretation of images
of pilgrimage in the on-going development of
Christian spirituality in the history of the Church,
we do not leave behind us the Scriptures of the Old
and New Testaments. Indeed, one may see the whole
of Christian history as an exegesis, in thought and
action, of the word of God. Or, perhaps, we might
even better call it an *eisegesis* – a 'reading in' of
ourselves into the word and will of God; a reading
of ourselves into the paradise of God, where, in a
fundamental and altogether crucial sense, we already
are.

Our concern now is with the spirituality of St
Augustine; but in order to preserve the continuity
of our theme, we should first attempt to place
him in the context of early Christian spirituality in
general. There are important differences there, and
significant development.

To begin with, it is not, of course, surprising that the Church should think of itself as representing paradise. St Irenaeus remarks: 'The Church is planted as a paradise in this world'.[33] Clearly, the Church, as community of the New Adam, and, indeed, of the New Eve (for that also is Irenaeus' thought),[34] the community in which the fraternal enmity of Cain and Abel is reversed by Christian amity, seems a return to Eden in this world. Thus, for the *Epistle to Diognetus*, those who love God rightly, have been made 'a paradise of delight'.[35] Theophilus of Antioch speaks expressly of redeemed man's return to Eden: '...with a kind of banishment (God) cast him out of paradise, so that through this punishment he might expiate his sin ... and after chastisement might later be recalled'.[36] The great Alexandrian doctors, Clement and Origen, speak of the consummation as the restoration of the primitive integrity: *Semper enim similis est finis initiis*, says Origen, 'the end is always like the beginning'; God 'will restore that state which rational nature possessed when there was no need of eating from the tree of knowledge of good and evil'.[37]

Although the return to paradise has an eschatological dimension, it is also present reality in the Church's life. As St Gregory of Nyssa remarks,

'It is indeed possible for us to return to the original beatitude, if we will now run backward on the same road which we had followed when we were ejected from Paradise together with our forefather [Adam]'.[38] The understanding of baptism as the sign of that return to paradise, the lost and promised land, is, of course, implicit from the beginning in the imagery of Exodus so closely associated with baptism in the Scriptures; but the point is dramatically underlined in early Christian liturgies, when the candidate's feet are washed, 'to wash off the venom of the serpent', [39] or when the newly baptized Christian is given milk mingled with honey, symbolic of the promised land.[40]

In early Christianity, the paradisal image serves as the fundamental image of renewal and reform, and thus it is the basic image of spiritual pilgrimage, in both individual and corporate dimensions. The biblical image is treated typologically: it is at once what it is in itself, historically, and also a foreshadowing of what is to come; it is *forma futuri, sacramentum futuri* – a sign of what is coming; and that on several levels. What is coming is fulfilled in the soul of redeemed man, in the community of the Church, and also in the summing-up which is the end of time; and thus it has always an eschatological dimension, eschatology both 'futurist' and 'realised'.

The reforming force of the paradisal image could be reflected in various and quite different ways. On the one hand, it might be seen, as by Eusebius, in the victory of the Christian Emperor, Constantine, turning a wilderness of lawlessness into a paradise of harmony, doing battle among '"thorns and briars," making peace and a "pleasant vineyard" after overcoming Satan'.[41] On the other hand, for the Desert Fathers, and for many others, seeking the *bios theoretikos*, the 'philosophic life', the integrity of paradise could be recovered only in the freedom of the wilderness, far removed from the affairs of the Imperial Church.[42] The aim was to recover in the wilderness the lost integrity of Adam; to show how Christian holiness could overcome the enmity of man and nature; and, of course, the lovely tales of tame lions and crocodiles, and repentant wolves, are simply charming illustrations of that point.

All that belonged to the imagery of paradise; but there was more. In the Latin West, in the fourth century, important changes were taking place in Christian spiritual perspectives; changes which would define Western Christian spirituality, through the Middle Ages, through the Reformation, down to our own time. St Augustine was the great architect of that transformation, although, of course, he did not actually invent it. It was somehow there before him; for instance, in the vast difference between Eusebius and Ambrose with regard to Christian emperors. And its roots were clearly biblical, most evidently in the Pauline theology of sin and grace. In this view, the paradisal image of reform means something different: not the return to the pristine integrity of Eden, however spiritually conceived. The integrity of Eden is not the pilgrim's destination: *In melius renovabimur*,[43] says St Augustine, 'we shall be changed into something better'. That is the watchword of this view.

I suppose the first clear patristic statement of this point belongs not to St Augustine, but to a slightly earlier document, sometimes ascribed to him: the traditional 'Paschal Praeconium', the 'Exultet' of the Easter Vigil, now pretty securely ascribed to St Augustine's great mentor, St Ambrose of Milan. I refer to the remarkable lines:

> O truly necessary sin of Adam, which by the death of Christ is done away! O happy fault, which merited such and so great a Redeemer![44]

One may recognise in that an echo of the Pauline doctrine, according to which, 'where sin abounded, grace did much more abound' (Rom. 5:20). But whatever may be the Pauline and Ambrosian anticipations of the position, its full elaboration belongs especially to St Augustine.

In the cyclic view of paradise as return to Eden, the wilderness must be seen as interlude, delaying our return to the innocent integrity of Adam in the garden. But if the New Adam is not just original integrity reconstituted, but something new and infinitely more, then wilderness is not just remedial discipline (though it is that, of course), but the sphere of spiritual activity which results in something better. *In melius renovabimur*: maturity in Christ is something more than the innocence of Adam. It is this latter view which specifies the terms of pilgrimage for St Augustine and his successors.

The spirituality of St Augustine is the spirituality of pilgrimage, and abounds in images of wilderness and paradise, of exile and repatriation.[45] This theme runs through all his works, but perhaps it is most familiar and most accessible in the *Confessions*, his own 'Odyssey of soul',[46] the story of his liberation from the futility of the social, educational and professional conventions of a dying age, from the 'barren land'[47] he had made of himself, to find a new principle of thought and action in the paradise of the word of God. Thus, the work, which begins as a sort of autobiography, turns into a consideration of the nature of the soul, and concludes as a meditation on the creation narrative of Genesis.

St Augustine's pilgrimage is the pilgrimage of *amor*, the pilgrimage of love, the spirituality of rational will, as it aspires to the infinite and absolute good. A passage in Book XIII of the *Confessions* clarifies the meaning of that journey:

By its own weight, a body inclines towards its own place. Weight does not always tend towards the lowest place, but to its own place. A stone falls, but fire rises. They move according to their own weights, they seek their own places. Oil poured into water rises to the surface; water poured on oil sinks below the oil. They act according to their own weights, they seek their own places. Things out of place are restless (*inquieta*); they find their places, and they rest.

My love is my weight (*Pondus meum amor meus*); whithersoever I am moved, I am moved there by love. By thy gift (*donum*, the

Holy Spirit) we are set on fire, and are borne aloft; we burn, and we are on the way. We climb the ascents which are in the heart, and sing the 'song of Degrees'.[48] With thy fire, with thy good fire, we burn and go on, for we go up to the 'peace of Jerusalem'; for I rejoiced in them who said to me, 'we will go into the house of the Lord'. There good will will place us, so that we shall wish nothing other than to remain there forever.[49]

In the realm of nature, motion has a necessary character; all created things, by their very natures, by their rising and decline, necessarily seek the good, in ordered and harmonious praise of God; but, in the human order, *amor* is the activity of rational will. It is precisely in the human will that St Augustine finds the possibility of a wayward love, which fixes upon some finite good as though that were the absolute and perfect good. *Amor*, self-blinded to the true object of its quest, becomes distorted, and perverted, and frustrated, and leads the soul to slavery: subservience to the sensible, to idle curiosity, and vain ambition, subject to all the demons of the 'present age'.[50]

Therefore, Augustinian spirituality has the character of a recovery from bondage, an Exodus from Egypt, the conversion of *amor* from finite goods to infinite and perfect good, which is the promised land of paradise, and the Prodigal's return from a distant country. The conversion, the ascent, is a movement away from the multiplicity and temporality of worldly experience, a turning inward in search of a vision of the unity and stability of all things in their divine source and end. The meaning of experience is not to be found in external phenomena, as such; they make sense only as they are judged and unified by the conscious self, in terms of principles of truth present to the soul. Turning inward, the soul discovers the presence of eternal Truth, transcending and illuminating, as the necessary pre-condition of its understanding. To see directly that eternal Truth, the ground of the being and intelligibility of all created things, and to know and love all things in that one Truth, and only there, is the final goal of the soul's ascent: the attainment of a beatitude of which the wayfaring soul has only proleptic glimpses.

There is much in that position which bears comparison with those spiritual traditions of ancient paganism we considered earlier. The whole pattern of the asceticism seems basically Platonic: from external things to the soul's own inner life, and from the soul to the soul's divine illuminating principle.

Surely, it is all there in Plato's great analogies of the Sun, the Line, and the Cave, in the *Republic*. Indeed, St Augustine himself informs us that he read, in the 'books of the Platonists', all this, and more. He tells us that he found there (in other words) much of the Prologue of St John's Gospel. But he did not read there, he says, that 'the word was made flesh and dwelt amongst us', that 'he came unto his own, and his own did not receive him', that 'to those who received him, he gave power to become sons of God'.[51] The similarities were striking; but the omissions were altogether crucial, because, as St Augustine understood it, the spiritual *impasse* of paganism lay precisely in the evident impossibility of any genuine mediation between the divine and human spheres. Without that *via*, the blessed homeland must remain only a vision, never an habitation.[52]

Only through the mediation of the Divine Word could Paradise become a home. The last three books of the *Confessions* are accordingly devoted to a meditation on the Eternal Word as the *principium* of creation, who is the illuminator of the soul, and also speaks to bodily senses in the words of Holy Scripture, that men immersed in sensible and temporal things might hear and believe that sensible and temporal word, and be recalled to find the truth within. Because of fallen man's preoccupation with external and temporal things, his memory of his *patria* is dim, and his *via* unclear, and therefore the prompting of the word, externally and temporally uttered, in the economy of salvation, is the necessary starting-point. [53]

Therefore, shunning the presumption which imperils merely human speculation about divine realities, St Augustine undertakes an exposition of the spiritual pilgrimage of all creation, in the form of an exegesis of the creation narrative of Genesis. First, creation is seen in its discursive multiplicity in time and space; finally, it is seen in its Sabbath-rest in the unfathomable unity of divine activity, in which motion and rest are identical. All things have been created from nothing, in dissimilitude to God; it is by a *conversio*, a turning back to God, that they attain the reality of their true life. That is the pilgrimage of all creation, the meaning of its motion, and it is within that context that the pilgrimage of human love is understood.

In melius renovabimur. I think it is important for us to see how sharply the spirituality of *amor* stands in contrast to the ideals of pagan spirituality. In the *City of God*, St Augustine speaks of the pagan myth of endlessly recurring cycles, [54] the *libridium*, the 'mockery', that immortal souls who have attained to wisdom are condemned to alternate endlessly between delusive blessedness and a misery which is genuine. He has in mind, no doubt, such stories as Plato's 'Myth of Er', and Virgil's account of Aeneas' journey to the underworld. 'By following the road of sound doctrine', says St Augustine, 'one escapes I know not what false cycles, invented by false and misled sages'. The Platonists can see, indeed, though in the distance, as it were, and with clouded vision, the *patria* which must be our home, but they do not hold to the *via* by which one must travel there. [55]

Criticising Virgil for the view that all our griefs and perturbations arise from the soul's incarceration in sluggish flesh, St Augustine insists that our ills are neither fated, nor circumstantial; it is the will, he says, the *amor*, which is all-important in the life of individual and community. [56] It is the principle of *amor* which informs the spirituality of St Augustine, and it is that principle which informs and shapes profoundly the new society which rises in the West from the ruins of the ancient Empire. It is the spirituality of *amor* which shapes medieval Christendom, for a millennium, to the late Middle Ages, and beyond, and defines the Christian pilgrimage in all its forms. It is that romantic spirituality which animates the infinite aspiration of medieval architecture and sculpture; it is that which animates the Marian devotions of St Anselm and St Bernard of Clairvaux; and it is the same spirituality, essentially, which informs the popular and vernacular literature of the age.

And that culminating work of medieval spiritual genius, the *Divine Comedy* of Dante, has the shape of romance, transfigured in the 'sweet new style', and fittingly concludes with the image of paradise as the white celestial rose, the image of purified romantic love; and the final line of the final canto celebrates *l'amor*: 'the love that moves the sun and the other stars'.

CHAPTER V

Dante

A rt and architecture, and, indeed, all the forms of Christian culture in the Middle Ages, abound in images of pilgrimage. One of the most striking architectural illustrations of our theme is the great twelfth-century basilica, Sainte-Marie-Madeleine, at Vézelay, in Burgundy. It was literally a pilgrimage church, both as the goal of pilgrimage, and as an assembly point for the great pilgrimage to St James at Compostella. It was there that St Bernard preached the Second Crusade, in 1147, and it was there that King Philip Augustus and Richard 'Coeur de Lion' mustered their forces for the journey to Jerusalem.

But the building speaks also of the inner pilgrimage of the Christian mind and heart, the soul's journey from darkness into light. Above the western portal of the nave, there is a great carved tympanum, announcing to the pilgrim the meaning of this place. The central figure is the cosmic

Christ, surrounded by foliage and water, flanked by twelve apostles and St Paul, upon whom the Holy Spirit's rays descend from the outstretched hands of Christ, commissioning them to go forth into all the world. A border shows all the varied peoples of the earth; and outside that, another border shows the signs of the zodiac, with all the varied forms of human labour.

Below that announcement of the meaning of the place, there is the figure of St John the Baptist, indicating the path of entrance. With astonishing architectural skill, the building is so oriented in its construction, that on St John the Baptist's Day the light from the clerestory windows makes a path of blocks of light precisely in the centre of the central aisle, from the dark narthex, right up the long and rather dimly lighted nave, straight to the altar, bathed in brilliant light. The pilgrim moves from darkness into light, from wilderness into paradise. The very structure of the building is an outward sign of the inner pilgrimage of spirit. As Abbot Suger put it, speaking of the dedication of the Abbey Church of St-Denis, in Paris, in 1140, 'That which is signified pleases more than that which signifies'. Inscribed upon the golden doors of St-Denis were the lines:

Bright is the noble work; but being nobly
bright, the work
Should brighten the minds, so that they may
travel through the true lights
To the True Light where Christ is the True
Door. [57]

In the works of Honorius Augustodunensis, one
of the most popular of medieval authors, the
symbolism of pilgrimage is thoroughly explicit
and all-encompassing. Sojourning man, forsaking
Egypt for the Promised Land, leaving Babylon for
Jerusalem, following a ten-fold path of all the liberal
and practical arts, comes to his true homeland, the
wisdom of the Scriptures. He attains that *superna
civitas*, the Heavenly Jerusalem, where wisdom
has prepared a banquet for her pilgrims, where
the *studiosi* ascend the mount of contemplation,
there to look upon Christ, with Moses and Elias, clad
in garments radiant as the sun. [58]

Medieval art and literature tell us much about
the spirit of the age. There is a light of glory there, in
those images of pilgrimage. It is true, of course, that
those who study Medieval Christendom will see that
there is also darkness there, and spiritual wickedness
in both high and low places; and when we look at

Dante, ' the voice (as Carlyle called him) of ten silent centuries', [59] we see both the dark and the light of it, the glory and the shame. Dante stands on the summit of Medieval Christendom, and displays all its lights and shades and subtleties. He is medieval, certainly, but he comes close, perhaps closest of all the poets and theologians, to a universal voice.

The great problem of the *Divine Comedy* for our present purposes is that the whole, vast work is about spiritual pilgrimage, about wilderness and paradise. To start with, even the dating of the work is significant. The theoretical date of the poet's journey is the year 1300, the year of Jubilee; because the subject of the work is spiritual liberation, release from Egyptian bondage, and the journey to the freedom of the Promised Land. [60] And the extent of the pilgrimage is just one week: from the night of Christ's betrayal to Thursday in Easter Week. These are, of course, points of the deepest significance for the interpretation of the work; but with amazing subtlety, Dante does not simply tell us these things. He lets them dawn upon our awareness gradually as we make our way through the work.

Dante's great poem presents itself on several levels: first of all, there are the great poetic images, Hell and Purgatory and Heaven, which specify the major divisions of the work; but they are poetic images, and the poem is not about those in any very direct way. It is about the universal pilgrimage of humankind, pagan and Christian man, in this earthly life, and it speaks about the conditions and the terms and the end of the journey. But finally, it is about the poet's own pilgrimage, the journey of his soul to God.

That pilgrimage is the task of everyman, and in another, earlier work, the *Convivio*, Dante describes its nature universally, and the reason for it:

Therefore, I say, that not only in gaining of knowledge and wealth, but in any acquisition whatsoever, human desire extends itself, in one way and another. And the reason is this: the deepest desire of each thing, arising from its very nature, is to return to its principle. And because God is the principle of our soul, and has made it like himself (as it is written, 'Let us make man in our image and likeness'), the soul mightily desires to turn to him.

And so, as a pilgrim (*peregrino*) who travels along a road he has not been on before, believes each building, seen in the distance, is the inn, and finding it not so, directs his belief to the next, and so from house to house, until at last he finds the inn; just so our soul, as soon as it enters upon the new and unfamiliar road of this life, directs its eyes towards the end, the highest good, and each thing it sees which manifests some good, it takes to be that end.

And because its knowledge is at first imperfect, inexperienced and untaught, little goods seem great to it, and thus it begins its longing first with them. Thus, we see infants intensely longing for an apple; and then, later on, for a little bird; and then, still further on, fine clothes; and then a horse; and then a mistress; then, modest riches; then more; and then still more. And that is because in none of these things does it find that which it ever seeks, and it believes to find it further on …

Indeed, we may lose the road by error, just as we may lose our way on earthly roads. Just as there is from one city to another one best and straightest road, and another which diverts us altogether (going in the opposite direction), and many others which divert

us more or less; so in human life there
are divers roads, of which one is the most
true, another most false, and others more
or less true or false. And just as we see that
the straightest road goes to the city, fulfills
our longing, and gives rest from toil, and
that the road which goes the opposite way
never achieves that end; so it is in our life,
that the good wayfarer (*lo bono camminatore*)
reaches the goal and has rest, while he who
goes astray never reaches it, but with great
agony of soul ever gazes onward with greedy
eyes.[61]

All that is implicit in the opening stanzas of the first
Canto of the 'Inferno', when the poet discovers
himself, 'in the middle of our life's road', lost in a
dark forest, wilderness (*selva selvaggia*), where the
true way has been abandoned. The goal still lies
before him, and he sees it in the distance: a mountain
mantled in the rays of morning sunlight; but as
he tries to make his way up the desert slope, he is
hindered and driven backward by a succession of
wild beasts – a leopard, a lion and a wolf, symbols of
the carelessness, violence and malice which impede
the progress of his soul. These beasts represent not

external force or circumstances, but passions of the soul, fantasies of vices, images of the wilderness within. [62]

The ghost of Virgil now appears upon the scene to aid the medieval poet in his desperation. Virgil, the voice of human reason and moral philosophy, explains to his frightened pupil that he cannot evade the beasts and climb directly up the mountain, but must approach it by another way, which will require a journey through the underworld, the wilderness of hell within his soul; he must come to understand the nature and the implications of his spiritual condition, symbolised by those beasts, those fantasies of vices. But the voice of reason will not move the pilgrim. He stands irresolute, until he hears that Virgil has been sent by Beatrice, who is the image of romantic love, and, ultimately, of the divine love. Only the knowledge of that love will permit the pilgrim to confront the reality of sin in all its implications.

The journey through the 'Inferno' is the story of the degradation already implicit in the poet's soul, but now spelled out, with penetrating logic, as he descends through ever-narrowing circles of hopelessness, carelessness, violence and malice. Nothing there is arbitrary: it is all the explication of his own condition. The journey ends with one of the most startling and brilliant of all of Dante's images: the very pit of hell, at the very centre of the earth, is not a fire, but a frozen lake, surrounded by giants (the ancient Titans), monstrous perversions of humanity. The wretched denizens who dwell within that final circle are those who have betrayed all ties of love, personal and social, now eternally consumed by Satan, represented as a monstrous perversion of the Holy Trinity.

The image of perdition as a frozen waste at the very centre of the earth serves the poet well: it is the image of the death of love. This is the point, says Dante, 'toward which all weight bears down from everywhere;' [63] at the centre of gravity, all weight is external. There is, then, no longer any inner weight of *amor*, no inner spring of personality. The 'good of intellect' is lost, and personality is dead. Surely no one in the whole history of literature has given so fiercely logical, so psychologically penetrating, so concretely illustrated an account of the nature and consequence of sin.

But if the lesson of the 'Inferno' is a weighty one, the 'Purgatorio' holds a still more weighty lesson. It begins on Easter morning, and its story is the story of the rebirth of love. The poetic image is a mountain, marked by seven cornices, representing the seven deadly sins, of which the pilgrim must be purged, as he pursues his quest for liberty, following commandment and example, and doing penance. It is the path of moral effort, attended by rigorous discipline, and many sermons.

At the summit of the mountain lies the 'Earthly Paradise'. It is the 'golden age' of Virgil, and the Eden of the Bible; it is the utopian dream of poets and philosophers, the harmony of man with man, and of man with nature. But remarkably, it has no residents; everything there has the form of allegory. It is the place of dreams and visions, and the place of revelation, but it is no resting-place. Eden is not, and cannot be the end of human aspiration. At best, it is only a beginning; at worst, it is a false and contradictory conclusion. 'Earthly Paradise' cannot substitute for heaven.

In this judgement, Dante stands clearly in the tradition of Western Christian spirituality. *In melius renovabimur*, said St Augustine, 'we shall be changed into something better', and St Thomas, who was Dante's chief spiritual guide, makes the same point, in the very first question of *The Summa Theologiae*, when he explains the necessity of supernatural revelation, on the grounds that human life is ordained toward God, as towards an end which exceeds the competence of human reason.[64] There is no intermediate stopping-place: *amor* which does not find its rest in God is everlastingly frustrated, and that is the spiritual condition described in the 'Inferno'.

An original and striking feature of Dante's 'Earthly Paradise' is the presence of two rivers there. First, there is the stream of 'Lethe', the waters of forgetfulness, familiar from the Elysium of Virgil, and of Plato; the waters which the souls must drink so as to forget the bliss of paradise and return to earthly life, in the endless cyclic pattern of aspiration and descent. For Dante, 'Lethe' has a different purpose: its point is to put away the stains of earthly sins. But even more remarkable is the meaning of the second stream, 'Eunoe'.

Commentators generally tell us that this word was coined by Dante from two Greek words, and means 'good memory', reversing the effect of 'Lethe'. But that must certainly be wrong. The word is rather Dante's adaptation of Aristotle's term *eunoia*, which Scholastic commentaries on the *Nicomachean Ethics*, with which Dante was certainly familiar, rendered as '*benevolentia*'. And as in Aristotle *eunoia* is the principle or starting-point of friendship, [65] here 'Eunoe' means divine benevolence, which is the principle of that divine and human friendship which St Thomas identifies as charity. [66] 'Eunoe' means the mediation of divine love in Christ, grace and revelation, first adumbrated for Dante in the love of Beatrice. Thus, the waters of 'Eunoe' must be the pilgrim's divinely-given preparation for the ascent to 'Paradiso':

> From those most holy waters, born anew
> I came, like trees by change of calendars
> Renewed with new-sprung foliage through and through,
>
> Pure and prepared to leap up to the stars. [67]

The 'Paradiso' represents, of course, the life of heaven. But, as with the 'Inferno' and the 'Purgatorio', it is not just a vision of the 'after-life', but a description of a spiritual condition in this life: a description of the pilgrim's road to heaven, and a representation of the heavenly life (the life of charity) on earth. Only the final cantos are a vision of the life of heaven as such.

The poetic image of the 'Paradiso' is astronomical: it is the system of the planetary and starry spheres, each with its specific grace and virtue, in a harmony of balance and reciprocity. The key to understanding its order and arrangement is the conception of charity as friendship. I must illustrate that point with reference to just one sphere, the heaven of the sun (symbol of intellectual light), in which we find the 'doctors', the teachers of sacred doctrine.[68] The doctors are arranged in two concentric circles, of twelve members each, captained, respectively, by St Thomas, the Dominican, and St Bonaventure, the Franciscan, whom Dante's contemporaries would recognise at once as representing rival orders, and different theological perspectives. The charity, the friendship and reciprocity of the arrangement is evident, as Dante gives to St Thomas the praises of St Francis, and to St Bonaventure the praises of St Dominic. The same point is emphasised within each circle, too. Thomas' circle includes, as its twelfth and last member (and therefore at his side) his notorious theological opponent, Sigier of Brabant. That speculative opposition within Thomas' circle is echoed in Bonaventure's circle by the presence there, in similar position, of Joachim of Fiore, whose spiritual teachings inspired the 'Spiritual Franciscans', and created immense practical difficulties for the Franciscan order, of which Bonaventure was Minister General. There are many other subtle balances and oppositions within the circles, [69] and between the circles, and between the different spheres of 'Paradiso'.

Dante's point is not to say that the differences are unimportant; but rather that in Christian intellectual and spiritual life, under the providence of God, the oppositions, embraced by charity, are essential to the harmony of the whole, just as in the musical scale (the music of the spheres), [70] both dissonance and consonance are essential. He employs the analogy of the 'Horloge' – the great astronomical clock, which was a new invention in Dante's time – in which the push and pull of weight and counter-weight are essential to the working of the whole. [71] And therefore,

No one should ever be too self-assured
In judgement like a farmer reckoning
His gains before the corn-crop is matured,

For I have seen the briar a prickly thing
And tough the winter through, and on its tip
Bearing the very rose at close of spring. [72]

Faith and hope and charity, which are the pilgrim virtues, must see the differences *sub specie aeternitatis*, in the perspective of eternity. Thus, as Dante approaches the last and broadest, all-inclusive sphere, 'the heaven of God's own quietude', his standpoint is reversed: he sees it as a burning point of light;[73] centre and circumference are one. That, and not the pit of hell, is the true centre of the universe. 'In that abyss', says Dante,

> I beheld how love held bound
> Into one volume all the leaves whose flight
> Is scattered through the universe around…
>
> For everything the will has ever sought
> Is gathered there, and there is every quest
> Made perfect, which apart from it falls short.[74]

Thus the 'Paradiso' ends with the poet's vision of the end of pilgrimage, in the love of God himself, the Holy Trinity:

> O thou eternal light, who dwellest in thyself alone,
> Alone self-knowing; joy and love proceed
> From thee, thy knower and thy known.[75]

And the poet sees this vision of the love of God *pinta de lo nostra effige*, 'painted with our (human) image'; it is the image of humanity, by virtue of the Incarnation, taken into God, into that love which, as the final line puts it, 'moves the sun and the other stars'.

CHAPTER VI

Reconciliation

Figures of wisdom back in the old sorrows
Hold and wait forever.
We see, admire
But never suffer them: suffer instead
A stubborn aberration.
O God, the fabulous wings unused,
Folded in the heart. [76]

With Dante's 'Paradiso', our pilgrimage through images of wilderness and paradise has come to a conclusion; but that is not to say that the pilgrimage just ends there. The images live in countless other representations, pagan and Christian, ancient, medieval and modern. [77] Many of the greatest works of modern literature would readily engender further chapters of our theme: one thinks immediately of Milton's *Paradise Lost* and *Paradise Regained*, Bunyan's *Pilgrim's Progress*, Rousseau's *Con-*

fessions, Goethe's *Faust* and *Wilhelm Meister*, and, in recent literature, of such works as Eliot's *Waste Land*, Kafka's *Metamorphosis*, Camus' *Stranger*, Sartre's *No Exit*, and so on.

What are all these, and countless others, but images of wilderness and paradise, Christian and pagan; paradise lost, paradise sought, paradise regained, or paradise impossible?

And it's not just the poets and the novelists: what, after all, is the spiritual substance of *Das Kapital*, but alienation, and repatriation to the harmonic bliss of a utopian paradise? The images are permanent features of our spiritual landscape, and we cannot think without them; they are witnesses of the restless heart, which has intimations of its homeland, and knows itself as a stranger and a pilgrim here.

The images are universal; but Christian thought and piety have a distinct understanding of them. As we have seen in our meditations on the Scriptures, St Augustine and Dante, there is a certain collation and reconciliation of the images, which constitutes the distinctive character of Christian spirituality. Paradise and wilderness are not just alternatives. Paradise is to come, certainly: 'Thy kingdom come', we pray; but at the same time, paradise is here, in the wilderness. Here we are fed with manna, the supersubstantial bread of heaven, for which we daily pray. Paradise is not just 'somewhere else', not just 'eastward in Eden'; it is, even here and now, 'a new heaven and a new earth', reconciled.

Christian spiritual life is neither 'this-worldly' nor 'other-worldly' – those are its temptations and distortions; authentically, it must be lived in the tension between those worlds, in the ambiguity between paradise attained and paradise to come. As St Paul explains it, all who are in Christ are, by the grace of God, new creations, [78] born anew, no longer at enmity with God, but friends of God. Our reconciliation has been accomplished, once for all; for Christ's sake, we are accounted friends of God. But, in another sense, our reconciliation is not complete, and will not be complete until our life of charity is finally fulfilled in the perfect knowledge and the perfect love of God; until, finally, 'we shall know as we are known'. Thus there is the tension between a justification, divinely-wrought, and finished once for all, and a sanctification which is being worked out within us day by day.

In that working out, the trials of the wilderness have a necessary place. Trials and temptations, the dark night of doubt, confusion and uncertainty, are not just unfortunate accidents. In God's good providence, they belong to the very life of faith, for faith must be tried, like precious metal, 'which from the earth is tried, and purified seven times in the fire'. [79] Perhaps those trials take different forms in one age or another, and different forms for each of us; but always they are, and must be there. Doubt and confusion – even the moment of betrayal – do not destroy the soul which is ready to return in penitence. What alone destroys the soul is the cold, hard cynicism which blasphemes against the Spirit; which simply doesn't care.

The trials of the wilderness are necessary, and must be embraced. Indeed, as St James puts it, we must 'count it all joy, knowing that the trial of your faith worketh patience. Let patience have her perfect work', he says, 'that ye may be perfect and entire'. [80]

Certainly the wilderness – the confusions of the world in which live, uncertainties within the Church, confusions within our own souls – certainly the wilderness presents us with problems and dilemmas, and it is surely not very easy to 'count it all joy', and discern and celebrate the lineaments of paradise within it. But that is precisely the nature of our calling, and, by the grace of God, who gives the

Bread of Life in the wilderness, we are not without resources to do just that.

We do possess, in faith, God's word of reconciliation, committed unto us. We do possess, in faith, God's work for us, God's word to us, made audible to us in Holy Scripture, made sensible to us in Holy Sacraments, if we will attend with minds and hearts obedient and penitent. We do possess, if we will, in the community of faith, centuries of wisdom and experience – none of it irrelevant – words and images of sanctity which will come alive for us, if we will give them (as to the shades in Homer's Hades) our own blood to drink. We do possess, in faith, an inner space of reconciliation, the knowledge of our justification, an inner space of peace and clarity, in which the Spirit teaches us the patience to look upon our trials *sub specie aeternitatis* – in the perspective of eternity. We do possess, in faith, a vision of the pure and perfect good, which is no mere vision, but our home; a vision in which all the scattered leaves of hopes and prophecies are bound together, as Dante says, into one volume, in the charity of God. [81]

We do possess, in the life of prayer, a bond which holds wilderness and paradise in one embrace. George Herbert, in *The Temple*, speaks wonderfully of that unitive way:

Prayer the church's banquet, angel's age,
God's breath in man returning to his birth,
The soul in paraphrase, heart in pilgrimage,
The Christian plummet sounding heav'n
        and earth
Engine against th' Almighty, sinner's tow'r,
Reversed thunder, Christ-side-piercing spear,
The six-days world transposing in an hour,
A kind of tune, which all things hear and fear;
Softness, and peace, and joy, and love,
        and bliss,
Exalted manna, gladness of the best,
Heaven in ordinary, man well drest,
The milky way, the bird of Paradise,
Church-bells beyond the stars heard,
        the soul's blood,
The land of spices; something understood

All this must be cultivated in the light of charity, that
best and highest gift of grace. Above all, charity. But
just what does that involve? The theologians tell us
that it is the form of all the virtues [83] – it includes and
shapes them all. And some of them are not easy for us
to bring together. Charity must include, for instance,
that obedience of mind whereby we stand firmly in
the truth, so far as we can see it; but it must also

include that humility of mind by which we recognise
that we know in part, and through a clouded mirror
which might benefit from some polishing. Then
also, it must include the more homely virtues of
cheerfulness, good-humour, and a readiness to think
well of one another. The fact is that we do not have it
all together. We have it in all the manifold diversity
of the Spirit's gifts; not as just one point of light, but
spread out among us, diversified. And therefore, if
we have charity at all, we have it in friendship and
reciprocity.

The practice of Christian spirituality presents
us, no doubt, with many difficulties. But only one
of those difficulties, I think, is really fundamental;
and that is the demoralising of the Christian mind
and heart, when we forget our pilgrimage and
fall into a mindless conformity to the spirit of the
present age, the *ambitio saeculi*, as St Augustine
(reading St John in the Latin version) calls
it.[84] Secular ideals, secular methods and measures
insidiously invade our consciousness, and pollute
the springs of spiritual life. We lose direction, and
we lose heart. We fall back into a hopeless neo-
pagan spirituality.

The only remedy – if we will trust it – lies
in the steady cultivation of the Christian virtues

of faith and hope and charity; holding on to the centuries of Christian wisdom, holding fast to our road of pilgrimage. What is essentially required is the practical upbuilding, among us and within us, of the life of penitential adoration. All depends, really, upon the prayerful life. St Bonaventure, one of the great masters of spirituality, in his book, *The Mind's Road to God* ('The Mendicant's Vision in the Wilderness' is its subtitle), puts it this way:

> Just as no one comes to wisdom save through grace, justice and knowledge, so none comes to contemplation save through penetrating meditation, holy conversation, and devout prayer. Just as grace is the foundation of the will's rectitude and of the enlightenment of clear and penetrating reason, so, first, we must pray; secondly, we must live holily; thirdly, we must strive toward the reflection of truth and, by our striving, mount step by step until we come to the high mountain where we shall see the God of gods in Sion. [85]

If we can follow such a recipe, surely we shall learn

that in the dark and stubborn forest which is our world and our very own souls, we find (as Dante says)[86] great good. We shall learn to bless our wildernesses, and thank God for them.

This year is the sixteen-hundredth anniversary of the conversion of St Augustine, that great exemplar of the Christian pilgrimage, upon whose works we have drawn so continually in these meditations, and we shall conclude now with a prayer from his *Confessions*:

Entering my secret chamber, I shall sing Thee songs of love, with groanings that cannot be uttered; in my pilgrimage remembering Jerusalem reaching out towards her with heart uplifted, Jerusalem my homeland, Jerusalem my mother. I shall remember Thee, her ruler, her illuminator, her father, her guardian, her spouse; Thee her pure and strong delight, Thee her solid joy, Thee all at once all goods ineffable, because Thou art the one true, highest Good.

I shall not turn aside until I reach that place of peace, Jerusalem, my dearest mother, where my first-fruits are already, whence comes my certitude; I shall not turn aside 'till Thou, my God, my Mercy, shalt gather in all that I am, from this dispersion and deformity, and conform it and confirm it in eternity. [87]

Notes

[1] Dante, *Divine Comedy*, 'Paradiso', XXXIII, 145: 'L'amor che move il sole e l'altre stelle'. Cf. Boethius, Consol., II, m. VIII:

> *O Felix hominum genus,*
> *Si vestros animos amor*
> *Quo caelum regitur regat.*

[2] On the place of images (metaphor) in Scripture, see St Thomas Aquinas, *Summa theol.*, I, 1, 9; for a discerning modern discussion of the same matter, see A. M. Farrer, *The Glass of Vision* (London, 1948).

[3] Cf. St Augustine, *Confessions*, XII, 28, and XIII.

[4] See especially M. Eliade, *The Quest: History and Meaning in Religion* (Chicago and London, 1969); 'The Yearning for Paradise in Primitive Tradition', in *Diogenes* (1959); and other works by the same author.

[5] St Augustine, *Confessions*, VII; *City of God*, passim; R. D. Crouse, 'Semina Rationum: St Augustine and

Boethius', *Dionysius*, 4 (1980), 75-86.

[6] Dante, *Divine Comedy*, 'Inferno', IV, 131.

[7] Homer, *Odyssey*, XXIV, 542-44 (trans. Robert Fitzgerald Garden City, N.Y., 1963), p. 462.

[8] Dante, *Divine Comedy*, 'Inferno', XXVI.

[9] Aristotle, *Nicomachean Ethics*, X, 7-8.

[10] Virgil, *Aeneid*, VI, 473-51 (trans. W. F. Jackson Knight, Virgil. *The Aeneid*, Harmondsworth, 1958), p. 169.

[11] St Gregory the Great, *Hom.* XXVIII (quoted by C. Dawson, 'The Dying World', in *St Augustine and his Age*, New York, 1957), p. 25.

[12] Dante, *Divine Comedy*, 'Inferno', XXVI.

[13] Homer, *Odyssey*, VII, 577-580 (tr. R. Fitzgerald, *op. cit.*, p.142).

[16] Homer, *Iliad*, XXIV, 527-32.

[15] Plato, *Republic*, II, 379d.

[16] Plato, *Republic*, X, 614b-520d. In *Republic*, X, 611, Plato speaks movingly of the soul's aspiration: 'our description of the soul is true of her present appearance; but we have seen her afflicted by countless evils, like the sea-god Glaucus, whose original form can hardly be discerned … But we must rather fix our eyes, Glaucon, on her love of wisdom and note how she seeks to apprehend and hold converse with the divine, immortal and everlasting world to which she is akin, and what she would become if her affections were entirely set on following the impulse which would lift her out of the

sea in which she is now sunken, and disencumber her of all that wild profusion of rock and shell, whose earthy substance has encrusted her, because she seeks what men call happiness by making earth her food.' tr. F. M. Cornford, *The Republic of Plato* (Oxford, 1941), pp. 345-46. Dante employs the Glaucus story to describe his own transformation upon entering paradise (Dante, *Divine Comedy*, 'Paradiso', I, 68-59).

[17] Romans 1:21.

[18] The use of Genesis in ancient catechetical instruction is still reflected in the structure of our traditional lectionary, where we begin the reading of Genesis at Septuagesima (once the beginning of Lent), as we prepare for our Lenten renewal of the spirit's pilgrimage.

[19] On the history of interpretation of the creation narrative, see *In Principio. Interprétations des premiers versets de la Genèse* (Paris, 1973); R. D. Crouse, '*Intentio Moysi*: Bede, Augustine, Eriugena and Plato in the *Hexaemeron* of Honorius Augustodunensis', *Dionysius*, 2 (1978), 137-157.

[20] Cf. St Augustine's interpretation of 'Heaven of Heavens', in *Confessions*, XII, 11-16.

[21] On the paradise of Eden as *forma futuri*, signifying Jerusalem, 'vision of peace', and the Church, see St Augustine, *De Genesi ad litteram*, XII, 56: '… *illo paradiso, ubi proprie fuit Adam, Ecclesia significata fit per formam futuri …. sicut Jerusalem, quae interpretatur*

visio Tacis, et tamen quaedam terrena civitas demonstrator, significat Jerusalem matrem nostram aeternam in caelis ...'.

[22] See, e.g., Dante's remarkable conflation of the imagery of Eden with that of Virgil's 'golden age', in '*la divina foresta*' of the 'Earthly Paradise', in Canto XXVIII of the 'Purgatorio'.

[23] St Augustine, *City of God*, XIV, 28: '*Fecerunt itaque civitates duas amores duo ...* '; also, *De Genesi ad litteram*, XI, 15.

[24] St Augustine, *City of God*, XIX, 5.

[25] Aristotle, *Nichomachean Ethics*, VIII. 7, 1159a; for Aristotle's comparison of divine and human life, see Metaphysics, XII, 7, 1072b. It is the opposition which Dante symbolises, on the eve of entering the 'Earthly Paradise', by his dream of Leah and Rachel ('Purgatorio', XXVII, 97 - 108).

[26] On divinely-given friendship, transforming friendship into charity, see St Thomas Aquinas, *Summa Theol.*, II, II, Q.XXIII: '*Unde manifestum est quod caritas amicitia quaedam est hominis ad deum.*'

[27] Cf. A.-J. Festugière, *Personal Religion among the Greeks* (Berkeley and Los Angeles, 1960).

[28] In what immediately follows, I have drawn upon the work of my friend and teacher, George H. Williams, *Wilderness and Paradise in Christian Thought* (New York, 1962), pp. 19-25.

[29] Rainer Maria Rilke, *Sonnets to Orpheus*, 9 (tr. C. F. MacIntyre, Berkeley and Los Angeles, 1961), p. 19.

[30] *The Apocalypse of Baruch* (ed. and tr. R. H. Charles, London, 1896, 77:13f; 29:8; 73:6), as quoted by G. H. Williams, *op. cit.*, p. 21.

[31] On the possible paradisal significance of the Marcan reference to 'wild beasts', see G. H. Williams., *op. cit.*, pp. 23-24.

[32] For a fuller description of the iconography, see Leonard Boyle, O. P., *A Short Guide to St Clement's, Rome* (4th ed., Rome, 1972), pp. 28-31.

[33] Irenaeus, *Adversus haeres*, V, 20, 2.

[34] On the Eva-Maria parallel, see Irenaeus, *Demonstration of the Apostolic Preaching*, 33; *Adv. haeres*, III, 32, 1, V, 19, I. The same parallel is found earlier in Justin Martyr (*Dialogue with Trypho*, 100), and later in Tertullian (*De carne Christi*, 17). For a full discussion of the matter, see Hugo Koch, *Virgo Eva – Virgo Maria* (ed. E. Hirsch and H. Leitzmann, Arbeiten zur Kirchengeschichte, 25, Berlin and Leipzig, 1937).

[35] *Epistle to Diognetus*, XII, 1; cf. Williams, *op. cit.*, p. 31.

[36] Theophilus of Antioch, *Ad Autolycum*, II, 26 (text and, translation by Robert M. Grant, Oxford, 1970, p. 69).

[37] Origen, *De principiis*, I, 6, 2; III, 6, 3 (tr. Gerhart B. Ladner, *The Idea of Reform. Its Impact on Christian Thought and Action in the Age of the Fathers* (Cambridge, Mass., 1959), p. 73. Ladner's section on 'The Return to Paradise' (in *The Greek Fathers*), pp. 63-82, is particularly relevant to our theme.

[38] Gregory of Nyssa, *De virginitate*, 12 (tr. Ladner, *op. cit.*, pp. 76-77).

[39] Ambrose, *De sacramentis*, III, I, 7: *'Lavas ergo pedes ut laves venena serpentis.'*

[40] Hippolytus, *Apostolic Tradition*, XXIII, 2. On the paradise theme in ancient Christian art, inscriptions and liturgy, see H. Leclercq, 'Paradis', in H. Leclercq, ed., *Dictionnaire d'archéologie chrétienne et de liturgie* Vol. XIII (Paris, 1937), coll. 1578-1615.

[41] Eusebius, *Life of Constantine*, III, 3, as glossed in Williams, *op. cit.*, p. 34.

[42] Cf. Williams, *op. cit.*, pp. 41-44.

[43] *De Genesi ad litteram*, VI, XX, 31 - VI, XXVIII, 40; quotation from VI, XXVII, 37: *In hoc ergo renovamur, secundum id quod amisit Adam, id est secundum spiritum mentis nostrae: secundum autem corpus quod seminatur animale, et resurget spiritale, in melius renovabimur, quod nondum fuit Adam.* See Ladner's excellent account of 'St Augustine and the Difference between the Reform Ideas of the Christian East and West', *op. cit.*, pp. 153-283.

[44] *O certe necessarium Adae peccatum, quod Christi morte deletum est! O felix culpa, quae talem ac tantum meruit habere Redemptorem!*

St Augustine evidently wrote a Paschal Praeconium, *in laude quadam cerei* (*City of God*, XV, 22), but the familiar one is almost certainly from St Ambrose; cf. B. Capelle, 'L'Exultet pascal, oeuvre de saint

Ambroise', in *Miscellanea Giovanni Mercati* (Vatican City, 1946), I, pp. 219-46.

45   For an excellent selection of texts in translation, with an introduction to 'The Spirituality of St Augustine', see Mary T. Clark, *Augustine of Hippo, Selected Writings* (Ramsey, N. J., 1984; in the series, 'Classics of Western Spirituality').

46   On the *Confessions* as 'pilgrimage', see G. N. Knauer, '*Pereginatio animae. Zur Frage der Einheit der augustinischen Konfessionen*', Hermes, 85 (1957-58), 216-248; R. J. O'Connell, *St Augustine's Confessions: The Odyssey of Soul* (Cambridge, Mass., 1969); R. D. Crouse, '*Recurrens in te unum*: The Pattern of St Augustine's *Confessions* in E. A. Livingstone, ed., *Studia Patristica*, vol. XIV (Berlin, 1976), pp. 389-92.

47   The 'barren land', *regio egestatis* (*Confessions*, II, X, 18) echoes the Latin text of St Luke, 15:14, and evokes the image of the Prodigal Son.

48   In the Latin Bible, Psalms 119-133 (KJV, 120-134), the 'Pilgrim Psalms', are entitled *canticum graduum*.

49   *Confessions*, XIII, 9, 10 (tr. R. D. C.).

50   Cf. R. D. Crouse, '*In multa defluximus*: *Confessions* X, 29-43, and St Augustine's Theory of Personality', in H. Blumenthal and R. Markus, eds., *Neoplatonism and Early Christian Thought* (London, 1980), pp. 180-85.

51   *Confessions*, VII, IX, 13.

52   *Confessions*, VII, XX, 26. On St Augustine's criticisms

of Platonism, in the *Confessions*, see C. J. Starnes, 'St Augustine and the Vision of the Truth', *Dionysius*, I (1977), 85-126; and, on the same matter in the *City of God*, Dennis House, 'St Augustine's Account of the Relation of Platonism to Christianity in the *De Civitate Dei*', *Dionysius*, VII (1983), 43-48.

[53]   *Confessions*, XI, VIII, 10.

[54]   *City of God*, XII, 14.

[55]   *City of God*, X, 29.

[56]   *City of God*, XIV, 5: '*Interest autem qualis sit voluntas hominis.*'

[57]   *Abbot Suger of the Abbey Church of St Denis and its Art Treasures*, ed. E. Panofsky, 2nd ed. Gerda Panofsky-Soergal (Princeton, 1979), p. 47. See also W. Beierwaltes, '*Negati Affirmatio*, or the World as Metaphor', *Dionysius*, 1 (1977), pp. 127-159.

[58]   Honorius Augustodunensis, *De animae exsilio et patria* (P. L., 172, 1241-1246); cf. R. D. Crouse, 'Honorius Augustodunensis: The Arts as *via ad patriam*', in *Arts Liberaux et philosophie au moyen age* (Paris and Montreal, 1969), pp. 531-539.

[59]   Thomas Carlyle, 'The Hero as Poet. Dante; Shakespeare', in W. Peacock, ed., *Selected English Essays* (Oxford, 1903), p. 366.

[60]   Cf. *Divine Comedy*, 'Purgatorio', II, 46, with its reference to the Easter Psalm (114), *In exitu Israel de Aegypto*; and Dante's exegesis of that Psalm in his 'Letter to Can Grande', *Epistola* XIII, 7.

[61] Dante, *Convivio*, IV, 12 (tr. R. D. C.).

[62] See, for instance, Honorius Augustodunensis, *op. cit.*, col. 1246: 'those who are devoted to transitory things will remain in exile, they will go into outer darkness, and, as with wounded eyes, flee eternal light eternally. But they encounter many and various fantasies of vices, as fierce beasts, which they wish always to escape, but never can avoid, because one after another they come upon them, and push them down into a vast pit of sorrow and desperation' (tr. R. D. C.).

[63] 'Inferno', XXXIV, 111.

[64] St Thomas Aquinas, *Summa theol.*, 1, 1, 1, resp.

[65] Aristotle, *Nicomachean Ethics*, IX, 5, 1167a.

[66] St Thomas Aquinas, *Summa theol.*, II, II, 23, 1, resp.

[67] 'Purgatorio', XXXIII, 142-145 (tr. Dorothy Sayers, in the Penguin edition of the *Divine Comedy*, which I take to be the most satisfactory of the many English translations, and most useful also for Dorothy Sayers' theologically astute notes).

[68] 'Paradiso', X - XIV.

[69] On the complex arrangement of doctors within the circles, see J.A. Doull, 'Dante on Averroism', *Actas del V Congeso Internacional de Filosofia Medieval*, I (Madrid, 1979), pp. 669-676; M. Bourbeau, 'La *doppia danza* du Paradis', *Dionysius*, 8 (1984), 105-130.

[70] 'Paradiso', I, 76-78.

[71] 'Paradiso', X, 139-148.

[72] 'Paradiso', XIII, 130-135 (tr. Sayers, *op. cit.*).

73 'Paradiso', XXVIII, 16-18; XXIX, 7-12.

74 'Paradiso', XXXIII, 85-87, 103-105 (tr. Sayers, *op. cit.*).

75 'Paradiso', XXXIII, 124-126 (tr. R. D. C.).

76 Christopher Fry, 'A Sleep of Prisoners', in *Three Plays* (London, 1960), p. 207.

77 Williams, *op. cit.*, for instance, traces the theme in the history of colonial New England, and also in the history of the idea of the university.

78 Romans, 5:17; cf. St Thomas Aquinas, *Super epistolas S. Pauli lectura, II ad Corinthios, IV*, 192.

79 Psalms, 12:6; I St Peter, 1:7.

80 St James, 1:3-4.

81 'Paradiso', XXXIII, 85-87.

82 George Herbert, 'Prayer', from *The Temple,* ed. J. Wall, George Herbert. *The Country Parson. The Temple* (Ramsey, N.J., 1981), pp. 165-66).

83 St Thomas Aquinas, *Summa theol.*, II, II, 23, 8; *De caritate*, 3.

84 I St John, 2:16; St Augustine, *Confessions*, X, 30; cf. R. D. Crouse, '*In multa defluximus: Confessions* X, 29-43, and St Augustine's Theory of Personality', in H. J. Blumenthal and R. A. Markus, eds., *Neoplatonism and Early Christian Thought* (London, 1981), pp. 180-85.

85 St Bonaventure, *Itinerarium mentis in Deum*, I, 8 (tr. G. Boas, St Bonaventure. *The Mind's Road to God*, Indianapolis and New York, 1953, p. 10).

86 'Inferno', I, 8.

87 St Augustine, *Confessions*, XII, 16, 23 (tr. R. D. C.).